WILLIAM ·MATHIAS

Learsongs

Settings of Edward Lear
for soprano and alto chorus
and piano duet

Music Department
OXFORD UNIVERSITY PRESS
Oxford and New York

Oxford University Press, Walton Street, Oxford OX2 6DP, England
Oxford University Press, 200 Madison Avenue, New York, NY 10016, USA

Oxford is a trade mark of Oxford University Press

© Oxford University Press 1992

This work was commissioned (with the financial support of the Welsh Arts Council) by the 1989 Toronto International Choral Festival, where it was first performed by the Toronto Children's Chorus conducted by Jean Ashworth Bartle.

Learsongs

Composer's Note

The nonsense poems of Edward Lear were an instant success on publication in nineteenth-century England, and they have since become part of the heritage of children all over the world. Some commentators have seen a deeper side to the poetry reflecting Lear's somewhat solitary life, and it is certainly true that for adults the humour has more than a tinge of melancholy. But his primary appeal is to children who understand the delightfully anarchic wit without any need for commentary.

Five of the best known poems are here selected to form a unified suite. The instrumental accompaniment is either for piano duet, or for a chamber group consisting of clarinet, trumpet, piano duet, percussion and double bass. This little 'cabaret band' combines with children's voices to create a particular sound world designed to reflect the uniquely humorous quality of Lear's poetic imagination.

W.M.

Duration – 15 minutes

The accompaniment for clarinet, trumpet, piano duet, percussion, and double bass is available from the Publisher's hire library

LEARSONGS

EDWARD LEAR
(1812 - 1888)

1. CALICO PIE

WILLIAM MATHIAS
(1988)

Lyrics:

Ca - li - co Pie, The lit - tle Birds fly Down to the ca - li - co tree, Their wings were blue, And they sang 'Til - ly - loo!' Till a-

OXFORD UNIVERSITY PRESS, MUSIC DEPARTMENT, WALTON STREET, OXFORD OX2 6DP

5

2. THE OWL AND THE PUSSY-CAT

Tur - key who lives on the hill. They dined on mince, and sli - ces of quince, Which they

Ah

Ah

ate with a run - ci -ble spoon; And hand in hand, on the edge of the sand, They

Ah

danced by the light of the moon, The moon, They danced by the light of the moon, The moon, They

Ah

Ah

danced by the light of the moon, The moon, They danced by the light of the moon.

Ah

3. THE DUCK AND THE KANGAROO

through! And we'd go to the Dee, and the Jel - ly Bo Lee,_____ O - ver the land, and

o - ver the sea;_ Please take me a ride! O do!'_____ Said the Duck to the Kan - ga - roo.

Said the Kan-ga-roo to the Duck, 'This re-quires some lit-tle re-flec-tion;___

Perhaps on the whole it might bring me luck, And there seems but one___ ob-jec-tion,___ Which is, if you'll let me

speak so bold, Your feet are un-pleas-ant-ly wet and cold, And would pro-ba-bly give me the roo-Ma-tiz!' said the

20

in the moon-light pale; But to ba - lance me well, dear Duck, sit stea - dy And

quite at the end of my tail!'_____ So a - way they went with a hop and a bound, And they hopped the whole world

three times round; And who so hap - py, _____ who, _____ who so hap - py, _____ who, _____

who so hap - py, ____ who, ____ As the Duck and the Kan - ga -

- roo? _____ roo? ____ roo? ____

4. UNCLE ARLY

O my a-ged Un-cle Ar-ly! Sit-ting on a heap of Bar-ley Thro' the si-lent hours of night, —

Close be-side a leaf-y thick-et: — On his nose there was a Crick-et, — In his hat a Rail-way-Tick-et;

(But his shoes were far too tight.)

Long a-go, in youth, he squan-der'd

He sub-sist-ed on those hills; — Whiles, — by teach-ing child-ren spell-ing, Or at times by mere-ly yell-ing, —

Ah

Ah

Ah

Or at in-ter-vals by sell-ing Prop-ter's Ni-co-de-mus Pills.' — La-ter, in his morn-ing ram-bles

Ah

Ah

He per-ceived the mov-ing bram-bles Some-thing square and white dis-close; — 'Twas a First-class Rail-way-Tick-et;

Ah

Ah

Ah

5. THE PELICAN CHORUS

By night we sleep on the cliffs a - bove;_____ By day we fish, and at

eve we stand_____ On long bare is - lands of yel - low sand.

S.

And when the sun sinks slow - ly down_____ And the great rock walls grow

A.

Ah_____ Ah_____

think so then, and we thought so still.

Ca - li - co Jam, The lit - tle Fish swam, O - ver the syl - la - bub sea, He took off his hat, To the

Sole and the Sprat, And the Wil-le-by-wat,— But he ne-ver came back, He ne-ver came back! He

ne-ver came back! He ne-ver came back to me!—

V

S.
Ploff-skin, Pluff-skin, Pe-li-can jee! We think no Birds so hap-py as we!

A.
Ploff-skin, Pluff-skin, Pe-li-can jee! We think no Birds so hap-py as we!

* Tutti clap (ad lib.)